GLOW UP LEADERSHIP

Lead Yourself First, Then Lead Everything Else

STEPHANIE WILLIAMS, MBA

WHERE HUSTLE MEETS STRATEGY

For permission requests, please contact:

Booked & Branded Publishing

www.bookedandbrandedpublishing.com

ISBN: 978-1-969369-21-6

Cover design, interior layout, and publishing by Booked & Branded Publishing.

This book should provide motivational and educational information on the subject covered. It is not a substitute for professional medical advice, diagnosis, or treatment. Always seek the advice of your physician or other qualified health provider with questions you may have regarding a medical condition.

Printed in the United States of America

Disclaimer

This book is for educational purposes only. It is not intended as legal, financial, or credit repair advice. While the strategies shared are based on the author's personal experience and research, results may vary depending on individual circumstances. Readers are encouraged to seek guidance from qualified financial professionals before making credit or financial decisions. The author and publisher disclaim any liability for any loss or damage resulting from the use of this information.

For permission requests, get in touch with the publisher: Booked and Branded Publishing.

Dedication

For the leaders who dared to go first — to heal first, when silence would have been easier.
To tell the truth first, when dishonesty would have been safer.
To set the standard first, when compromise would have been more convenient.
This book is for the leaders who understand that culture is not created by slogans, posters, or speeches—it is made by choices, by character, and by consistency.
You are the culture.
You are an example.
You are the spark that shows others what is possible.
And because you went first, generations after you will walk further, lead stronger, and live freer.

About the Author

Stephanie Williams, MBA — Strategic Business Consultant, author, and builder of beauty, brains, and business.

Stephanie Williams is a powerhouse in strategy, leadership, and transformation. With a perfect GPA from the prestigious Jack Welch Management Institute, where she earned her MBA with a concentration in Entrepreneurship, Stephanie has built her career helping individuals and organizations turn vision into results.

From her success in corporate sales at Verizon to founding Booked & Branded Publishing, a luxury ghostwriting and publishing firm, Stephanie has consistently proven her ability to lead, execute, and scale. Her work spans industries — from real estate and trucking to skincare and leadership — reflecting both her business acumen and her passion for empowering others to reach their next level.

In Glow Up Leadership: Lead Yourself First, Then Lead Everything Else, Stephanie combines her real-world experience with a relatable, motivational voice that makes leadership accessible without watering it down. She believes authentic leadership starts with self-mastery — building confidence, clarity, and consistency — and then flows into every team, project, or business you touch.

Through her books, coaching, and publishing company, Stephanie's mission is simple: to help leaders glow from the inside out, leading lives and organizations that are not only successful, but sustainable, authentic, and impactful.

Stephanie lives by the mantra: "Where hustle meets strategy." This philosophy influences both her personal journey and her mission to empower others to build legacies with purpose, clarity, and impact.

Booked & Branded Publishing

Table of Contents

Introduction

Leadership is not a title you wait to be given—it is a discipline you choose to master. Every day, the world is filled with managers who maintain, supervisors who monitor, and executives who execute. But genuine leaders? They do something different. They set standards, create futures, and leave legacies.

This book is not about teaching you how to look like a leader. It's about transforming you into the person others trust to follow—because of your consistency, your courage, and your clarity.

I wrote this book for ambitious professionals, entrepreneurs, and executives who know that success alone is not enough. You don't just want results—you want **impact that endures.** You want to lead teams that thrive, businesses that scale, and lives that inspire. You want to glow up as a leader—not just in what you do, but in who you become.

Inside these pages, you'll learn:

- How to master yourself before you attempt to lead anyone else.
- How to build authentic confidence that silences imposter thoughts.
- How to cast a vision so vivid that others want to step into it with you.
- How to communicate with authority, clarity, and influence.

- How to build teams, navigate conflict, and decide under pressure.
- How to lead not only for today's success, but for tomorrow's legacy.

Each chapter is layered with **frameworks, strategies, and power prompts you can** immediately apply in your leadership journey. The tone is direct, practical, and uncompromising—because your influence deserves more than vague inspiration.

This is not a book of theories. It is a **field guide for leaders who are serious about building legacies.**

So as you begin, I invite you to do something radical: approach this book not as information, but as a transformation. Don't just read it—practice it. Don't just highlight it—apply it. Don't just quote it—live it.

Because when you lead yourself first—your time, your standards, your emotions—you unlock the credibility and capacity to lead everything else.

Welcome to Glow Up Leadership. Where hustle meets strategy, and where success strengthens into legacy.

CHAPTER 1

The Foundation: Leading Yourself First

L eadership does not begin with titles, positions, or even vision boards. It starts with the person staring back at you in the mirror each morning. If you cannot lead yourself with clarity, discipline, and integrity, every team you touch will inherit the cracks in your foundation. Authentic leadership starts in private long before it has displayed in public.

Many ambitious professionals mistakenly believe leadership is primarily about managing others. What is the truth? The culture you build externally is only a reflection of the standards you uphold internally. If your calendar is chaotic, your energy undisciplined, and your promises broken—even silently to yourself—your influence will always leak.

To direct oneself properly is not a motivational slogan. It is a **system of self-governance**—a rhythm of discipline that ensures your life is aligned with your mission.

The Three Pillars of Self-Leadership

1. Identity — Who You Are When No One Is Watching

Your true identity shows up in the quiet, hidden places. It is the voice you use when you fail, the honesty you practice when shortcuts tempt you, and the values you choose when compromise would be easier. High-level leaders anchor their choices in a clear sense of who they are becoming—not just what they are producing.

Luxury Lens: Ask yourself, *would I respect this version of me if I were my mentor?* Identity is the filter that determines whether you attract respect or demand it.

2. Integrity — Keeping Promises to Yourself

Most people think about integrity only to keep promises to others. But elite leaders know the deeper test: *Do I keep the small, boring promises I've made to myself?* Waking up on time, finishing the workout, preparing the meeting notes—these micro-commitments build invisible credibility.

Over time, integrity compounds into trust. And trust—especially self-trust—is the most valuable currency you can possess as a leader.

3. Implementation — Turning Priorities Into Behaviors

Ideas are abundant. Implementation is rare. The difference between leaders who glow and leaders who burn out is not brilliance—it's consistency. A flawless plan that is not executed produces nothing; an average plan executed daily creates momentum that compounds.

Luxury leadership is not about occasional bursts of brilliance. It is about designing daily habits that make extraordinary results inevitable.

A Simple Leader's Operating System (LOS)

Every legacy-minded leader needs a practical, repeatable rhythm that governs their day. Below is a framework that ensures your leadership starts aligned and ends accountable:

- Morning (30–60 minutes):
  - Clarity check: what are the three outcomes today that truly move the mission forward?
  - Energy check: Did I invest in at least one physical input—sleep, hydration, protein, or movement—before 9 a.m.?
  - Courage check: Which conversation am I avoiding that, if addressed, would unlock momentum?
- Midday (10 minutes):
  - Re-align to outcomes. If you're busy but not advancing the mission, you're hiding in tasks.
  - Evening (15 minutes):
  - *Truth audit:* What was the most honest decision I made today? What did I postpone, and why?
  - *Future alignment:* Convert tomorrow's top three outcomes into calendar blocks now—don't leave your priorities to chance.

This system is not about micromanaging every hour. It's about ensuring that your time, energy, and courage are directed where they create the highest return.

The Mirror Test

Ask yourself: *If my team mirrored my habits for 90 days, would I be proud of the culture we create?* If the answer is no, don't rush to change your team—change yourself first.

Remember, culture is never what you write on the walls or post on LinkedIn. Culture is what you model when no one is watching.

Practical Example: The CEO's Calendar

I once advised a CEO whose company had grown rapidly but whose team was collapsing under chaos. When I reviewed his calendar, I noticed it was filled with back-to-back meetings and urgent requests—but none of the strategic blocks he claimed were his "top priorities." His culture mirrored him: reactive, scattered, and exhausted.

We restructured his schedule around the Leader's Operating System. Within 60 days, not only did his energy improve, but his team also began blocking their own deep-work times, courageously tackling tough conversations, and aligning daily outputs with quarterly outcomes. His leadership didn't change because he issued a new memo—it changed because he changed his habits.

Power Prompts

- What promise to myself, if kept for the next 30 days, would build the deepest reservoir of self-trust?
- Where am I relying on raw talent to compensate for a lack of structure—and how can I replace talent with systems?
- If my leadership legacy started today, would I be proud of how I use my mornings, my energy, and my courage?

Final Word on the Foundation

Leadership is never built in a single breakthrough moment. It is built on quiet, consistent decisions that compound over weeks, months, and years. The world doesn't just need leaders who can deliver results—it needs leaders who embody discipline, integrity, and courage when no one is applauding.

Before you ask others to trust you with their future, prove that you can trust yourself with your own. That is the foundation.

CHAPTER 2

Authentic Confidence vs. Performance Confidence

There is a reason some leaders radiate presence while others chase applause. The difference is not charisma—it's confidence. But not all confidence is created equal.

Performance confidence is loud, fragile, and dependent on external validation. It thrives on applause, titles, and comparison. It can look impressive but collapse quickly under scrutiny.

Authentic confidence, however, is quieter but unshakable. It is rooted in preparation, alignment, and internal trust. It doesn't require attention to matter, because it is built from within.

Luxury leaders know that the type of confidence you build determines whether you burn out chasing recognition—or glow up by leading from alignment.

The Confidence Continuum

Every leader lives somewhere along this spectrum:

1. **Insecure Performance**
   o Driven by masks, perfectionism, and constant comparison.
   o The leader always needs to "prove" something, whether through long hours, inflated titles, or excessive control.
   o Teams sense the instability and mirror the insecurity with their own stress and hesitation.

2. **Transitional Confidence**
   o Competent but inconsistent. When things are going well, it resembles fortitude.
   o These leaders often know their potential but haven't yet built consistent systems to sustain their confidence.

3. **Authentic Confidence**
   o The gold standard: competence combined with preparation, anchored in personal values.
   o This leader doesn't just act confident—they *are* confident because their actions, habits, and standards are aligned with their purpose.

Building Authentic Confidence: The C.A.L.M. Method

Confidence isn't magic—it's built like muscle. The **C.A.L.M. Method** is a practical framework for developing confidence that can withstand pressure.

- **C — Competence.**
  - o Study your domain until you are *unconfusable.* High-level leaders block 60–90 minutes each week to go deeper than their current role requires. Competence is not about knowing everything— it's about knowing enough that no curveball can destabilize you.
- **A — Action Reps.**
  - o The brain trusts what it repeats. Confidence grows from action, not theory. Record how many negotiations, pitches, or feedback conversations you complete—not just how many you prepare for. Volume builds calm.
- **L — Low-Ego Review.**
  - o After every key moment, ask, *"What worked? What will I do differently next time?"* Notice that the question is not, *"Was I good?"* Performance- focused leaders obsess over appearances. Authentic leaders measure growth.
- **M — Meaning.**
  - o Tie your work to who you are becoming, not just what you are producing. Meaning transforms tasks into legacy. When your confidence is connected to a mission larger than yourself, it becomes unshakable.

Kill the Costume

Performance confidence often comes dressed in costumes—grand speeches, jargon-filled reports, or flashy slides. But the most respected leaders are those who strip away performance and replace it with clarity.

In meetings, trade long preambles for clear, helpful contributions.

- "Here's the aim."
- "Here's what we tried."
- "Here's what the data says."
- "Here's my recommendation."

This shift from performance to service signals authority. It shows your team and peers that you are not chasing recognition—you are delivering value.

Practical Example: The Executive Who Stopped Performing

I once coached a senior executive who spent hours rehearsing how to "look confident" before board meetings. He remembered every detail, but his speech appeared unnatural and his presence stiff. The board respected his knowledge but didn't fully trust his leadership.

We shifted his focus. Instead of trying to *look impressive*, he practiced *being useful*. Each presentation was reframed into four sentences: the aim, the attempt, the data, and the recommendation. Within two months, his reputation transformed. The board stopped commenting on his delivery style and started leaning on his clarity for decision-making. His authentic confidence outweighed his need for performance.

Power Prompts

- Where am I performing instead of serving?
- What skill, if mastered, would quiet 80% of my imposter thoughts?
- If all applause were removed tomorrow, would I still trust my preparation?

Final Word on Confidence

Authentic confidence is not about noise—it's about foundation. It is the steady posture that comes from knowing who you are, preparing intensely, and aligning your work with purpose.

Performance fades when the applause ends. Authentic confidence compounds every time you honor your preparation, serve instead of perform, and connect your work to a mission that outlives you.

CHAPTER 3

Vision Casting: Seeing Beyond Today

Managers optimize the present. They refine processes, track metrics, and ensure tasks are completed. Leaders, however, operate in a different dimension. They create the future, then invite others into it. A leader without vision may succeed in the short term, but they will eventually plateau. A leader with vision builds organizations, movements, and legacies that outlive their own tenure.

Vision is not a motivational slogan—it is a leadership operating system. It aligns teams, drives focus, and creates momentum. Without vision, effort fragments. With vision, effort compounds.

The Anatomy of a Vision

A vision that inspires action has three essential ingredients:

1. A Picture — Specific and Vivid

A vague statement like *"We'll be better"* does not move people. A vision must be painted with such detail that others can almost see it. For example: *"A 24-hour turnaround on client drafts with measurable quality metrics and client satisfaction scores above 90%."* Clarity fuels alignment.

2. A Path — Milestones, Not Miracles

Vision is not a miracle waiting to happen—it is a sequence of intentional steps. Milestones break the future into achievable phases. They reassure your team that the dream is not a fantasy, but a roadmap.

3. A Purpose — Beyond Revenue

Revenue sustains the organization, but purpose sustains the people. Teams are energized when they understand *why* their work matters beyond numbers. Purpose is the bridge between the task in front of them and the legacy they are building.

The V.I.S.I.O.N. Framework

To move from concept to clarity, apply the V.I.S.I.O.N. framework:

- **V — Vivid:**
  Paint it like a scene. Don't say, "We'll improve customer service." Say, "By Q2, every customer email will be answered within six hours with a personalized solution, not a template."

- **I — Instructive:**
  Spell out behavior shifts. How will your team *act differently* under this vision?
- **S — Sequenced:**
  Map the journey in phases—30/60/90 days leading into a 12-month arc. People commit more fully when they see progress checkpoints.
- **I — Inclusive:**
  Assign ownership. A vision that belongs only to the leader dies quickly. A vision owned collectively lives longer.
- **O — Observable:**
  Define proof. What metrics, leading indicators, or customer outcomes will show progress? If it can't be measured, it will be neglected.
- **N — Narrative:**
  Wrap it in a story. Data explains, but stories inspire. Tell your vision like a narrative your people can remember and repeat.

The 90-Day Vision Sprint

The fastest way to build credibility with vision is to prove progress quickly. Enter the 90-Day Vision Sprint—a practical framework to turn vision into reality.

- **Days 1–7: Baseline Reality.**
  Define where you are. Capture the truth, even if it's uncomfortable. Then, identify three leverage moves that—if improved—would create the most impact.

- **Days 8–30: Pilot.**
  Test those moves in small, controlled environments. Collect feedback aggressively. Piloting reduces risk and builds early wins.
- **Days 31–60: Scale.**
  Expand what's working. Remove what isn't. Communicate progress consistently to reinforce belief in the vision.
- **Days 61–90: Standardize.**
  Lock in the systems—document playbooks, create training, and ensure the new practices survive without constant supervision.

This sprint doesn't replace the long-term vision. It speeds up belief by showing progress quickly—proof that the future is not just imagined but being built.

Practical Example: Vision in Action

I once worked with a healthcare startup struggling to motivate its clinical team. Their initial "vision" was vague: *"We want to revolutionize patient care."* Inspiring words, but too abstract to drive daily behavior.

We reframed the vision using the V.I.S.I.O.N. framework: *"Within 90 days, every patient will leave with a same-day care plan, digitally accessible within three clicks, with 95% patient satisfaction scores."*

The result? Staff knew exactly what the future looked like, what milestones to hit, who owned which steps, and how success would be measured. Within three months, the team not only hit the target—they became evangelists for the new system. The vision stopped being abstract and became culture.

Power Prompts

- If we only did three things in the next 90 days, which would bend the future the most?
- What are we doing now that future-us would immediately stop?
- Can my team describe our vision in one sentence, without me in the room?

Final Word on Vision

Vision is not reserved for the most charismatic leaders—it is available to anyone disciplined enough to imagine clearly, plan intentionally, and communicate consistently. A leader without vision manages the present. A leader with vision reshapes the future.

Your legacy will not be measured only by what you accomplish today, but by the future you dared to design and the people you had the wisdom to invite into it.

CHAPTER 4

Emotional Intelligence: The Heartbeat of Leadership

S trategy alone does not build trust. Systems alone do not create loyalty. The actual heartbeat of leadership is **emotional intelligence (EQ)**—the ability to understand yourself, regulate your emotions, and connect meaningfully with others.

Lacking EQ, even brilliant strategies collapse as individuals never have enough security to share honesty. And safety is not softness. Safety is a condition for honesty. It is the invisible infrastructure that allows information to flow freely, mistakes to be addressed quickly, and innovation to surface consistently.

Elite executives get this: when individuals have a sense of psychological safety, they offer their top concepts, question beliefs, and remain involved. When they don't, they retreat into silence, self-protection, and passive compliance.

The Four Moves of EQ

1. Self-Awareness — Notice Your Nervous System

Emotional intelligence begins with noticing yourself. Are you in fight, flight, freeze, or fawn mode? A leader who is unaware of their inner state will unconsciously project stress onto their team. Awareness creates choice. The more quickly you recognize your state, the faster you can recalibrate.

Luxury Practice: Journal daily on what triggered you most and how you responded. Over time, you'll recognize patterns that allow you to intervene earlier.

2. Self-Management — Pause Before You Lead

Awareness without discipline creates volatility. Top executives become skilled at the pause: breathe, identify the emotion, and then select the reaction. A leader who can regulate under pressure becomes a stabilizer in moments when others spiral.

Example: Instead of snapping at a missed deadline, the disciplined leader asks, *"What got in the way?"*—seeking clarity before judgment.

3. Social Awareness — Read the Room

Leadership requires antennae tuned not only to the spoken words but also to the unspoken signals. Energy levels, body language, and subtle disengagement often reveal the actual story. Social awareness enables leaders to see risks, opportunities, and resistance before they become crises.

Mentor's Insight: If a once-engaged employee goes quiet in meetings, don't assume agreement—assume untold concerns. Ask privately, *"What's not being said here?"*

4. **Relationship Management — Deliver Truth with Care**

   Prominent leaders do not avoid hard truths—they deliver them in ways people can receive. That is the essence of relationship management. A standard without support becomes cruelty; support without a standard becomes coddling. Authentic leadership balances both.

The 3-Sentence Feedback Script

Feedback should never be vague or punitive. It should be clear, constructive, and actionable. This simple framework ensures feedback is both firm and supportive.

1. "What I'm seeing/what happened is ____."
2. "The impact is ____."
3. "Here's the standard and the support I'll provide."

Close with a question: "What do you need to meet this?"
   This script respects dignity while reinforcing accountability. It creates dialogue rather than defensiveness.

Psychological Safety in Practice

Managers often assess security within their teams too highly.

Psychological safety isn't about comfort—it's about creating the conditions where people can risk honesty without fearing retribution.

- **Begin Meetings with Structure.**
  Start every meeting with context, desired outcome, and a time check. Structure reduces anxiety and signals respect for people's time.
- **Normalize Red Flags.**
  Invite dissent openly. Say: *"Tell me what I'm missing."* A single moment of dissent can prevent months of wasted effort.
- **Debrief Without Shame.**
  When things go wrong, resist blaming. Debrief using this sequence: facts → impact → next time. This ensures learning without humiliation.

Practical Example: The Team That Spoke Up

I worked with a technology company where team members rarely voiced concerns. Deadlines were missed, yet silence dominated meetings. After implementing psychological safety practices—such as inviting dissent, using structured debriefs, and providing feedback with the 3-sentence script—something shifted.

Within weeks, engineers began flagging risks earlier, saving the company both time and money. The CEO later admitted, *"I thought silence meant agreement. I now know silence was fear."* That awareness transformed not just the culture, but the business outcomes.

Power Prompts

- Where has my silence created confusion?
- Which relationship in my sphere needs honest repair this week?
- If my team were candid with me, what truth might I hear tomorrow?

Final Word on EQ

Emotional intelligence is not optional—it is the hidden infrastructure of sustainable leadership. Without it, leaders may achieve results but lose trust. With it, leaders create cultures where people not only perform but also thrive.

When strategy fails, look for the absence of safety. When vision fades, look for the lack of honesty. And when leadership breaks down, look for the absence of emotional intelligence. The strongest leaders are not those who know the most, but those who create environments where others can tell the truth, take risks, and grow.

CHAPTER 5

Communication That Inspires Action

Your words are not just tools—they are culture in transit. Every message you send, every meeting you lead, every announcement you make carries the DNA of your leadership. If your words are simple, confident, and interesting, your culture will reflect it. If they are vague, scattered, or uninspiring, your culture will echo that as well.

Luxury leaders understand that communication is not about sounding smart—it is about creating alignment. Clarity builds speed. Concise writing builds focus. Interesting messages build momentum. When your communication inspires action, you transform words into results.

The 4C Model for Every Message

High-level leaders discipline themselves to filter every message through four dimensions:

1. Clear — Plain Language, One Main Point

Complexity confuses—simplicity scales. Instead of hiding behind jargon, communicate with precision: one central point, one clear aim.

Example: Instead of "Our operational efficiency requires significant optimization across functions," say "We need to reduce client onboarding time from 14 days to 7 days."

2. Concise — Short and Direct

Respect attention spans. Use brief paragraphs, bullets, and time-boxing. Excellent communication is not about how much you say—it's about how little you need to speak to move the mission forward.

3. Concrete — Numbers, Next Steps, Names

Abstractions inspire briefly; concreteness inspires consistently. Always define outcomes with specifics. Who owns it? When is it due? What are the measurable targets?

4. Interesting — Why This Matters Now

A sense of haste without meaning is like pressure. Significance, lacking a sense of immediacy, is dismissible. The best communicators combine both. The mission provides a base for the "why," making each message seem needed and important.

Architecture Session (30–45 Minutes)

Meetings often waste energy because they lack structure. Luxury leaders treat meetings as investments and demand a clear return. Here is a blueprint for a high-affected 30–45 minute meeting:

1. **5 Minutes: Outcome + Agenda**
   Frame the purpose. Define success before the conversation begins.

2. **20–25 Minutes: Decisions + Blockers**
   Focus only on what moves the mission. Owners present recommendations, not problems. The rule is: *"If you don't have a recommendation, you don't have a presentation."*

3. **5–10 Minutes: Confirm Who Does What by When**
   Every decision must have an owner, a timeline, and accountability. Without this step, meetings become entertainment, not execution.

4. **3–5 Minutes: Risks + Gratitude + Recap in Writing**
   Highlight potential pitfalls, acknowledge contributions, and send a written recap. This makes people responsible and ensures the task is finished.

Write to Lead

Putting words onto the page is leadership. In emails, memos, or messages, you can either create alignment or chaos. Use these principles to ensure your words lead with authority:

- **Use "because" to Anchor Logic.**
  Explanations reduce resistance. People trust decisions more when they understand the reason behind them.
- **Move the passive to active.**
  Replace "The project will be completed by Friday," with "We will complete the project by Friday." The active voice signals ownership and commitment.
- **End with a verb.**
  Every message should direct action. Instead of ending with ambiguity, give a clear next step: *"Reply with 'approved' or 'needs change.'"*

Practical Example: Communication that Saved a Launch

A luxury retail brand once faced chaos in preparing for a significant product launch. Emails were long, unclear, and overloaded with jargon. Team members worked hard but were misaligned, missing deadlines and duplicating tasks.

We implemented the **4C model**. Every message had one point, one owner, one deadline, and a clear "why." Within two weeks, communication improved dramatically. Meetings were shortened by half, execution was sped up, and the launch not only happened on time—it exceeded sales projections by 30%.

The brand didn't just gain revenue. It gained a culture of clarity.

Power Prompts

- If this message were the only thing someone saw today, would they know the goal, the owner, and the deadline?
- What can I cut without losing meaning?
- Is my communication similar to a command—or a welcome to unite with something bigger?

Final Word on Communication

Communication is the currency of leadership. Every word you speak or write either deposits clarity or withdraws trust. Leaders whose primary communication build speed, alignment, and loyalty. Leaders who neglect it create confusion, hesitation, and wasted effort.

If your words carry weight, your culture will have momentum. Communicate not just to inform—but to inspire action. That is the mark of a leader whose influence endures.

CHAPTER 6

Boundaries, Balance, and Burnout Prevention

Burnout is not a badge of honor—it is a bill that always comes due. Leaders who ignore boundaries and balance eventually pay with their health, relationships, or credibility. The choice is simple: either you protect your energy early with rest and structure, or you will pay for it later with exhaustion, turnover, and decline.

Luxury leaders understand boundaries are not restrictions—they are systems that protect excellence. Balance is not about doing less—it is about directing energy where it matters most. Burnout prevention is not about weakness—it is about preserving longevity so you can lead at a high level for decades, not months.

The Non-Negotiables

Elite leaders establish non-negotiables around **time, energy, and attention.** These are not suggestions—they are standards.

1. Time

Guard your calendar with the same discipline you guard your finances—block hours for deep work, recovery, and strategic thinking. If your calendar is always available, your leadership will always be reactive.

Mentor's Insight: The most successful executives schedule "white space" for creativity, reflection, and strategy. Without this, they become operators trapped in busyness instead of architects building the future.

2. Energy

Movement, hydration, sunlight, and protein are not luxuries—they are fuel. Leaders who neglect their physiology sabotage their leadership capacity. If your body is depleted, your decisions suffer.

Practice: Treat physical inputs like boardroom priorities. Hydrate before every meeting. Stand or walk during calls. Protect sleep as fiercely as a financial asset.

3. Attention

Attention is the most valuable currency you control. Eliminate distractions before they eliminate your focus. Turn off non-critical notifications. Curate your digital environment as carefully as an athlete designs a training plan.

The B.O.L.D. Boundary Script

Leaders often hesitate to enforce boundaries for fear of disappointing others. But clear, respectful boundaries build trust. Use the **B.O.L.D. framework** to communicate them with authority:

- **B — Begin with Context:** "To protect delivery quality..."
- **O — Offer the Standard:** "I need 24 hours for review."
- **L — List Support:** "If urgent, text 'red' and I'll triage."
- **D — Decide the Outcome:** "If we miss the window, it moves to Monday."

This approach prevents resentment by pairing high standards with clear support. Boundaries are not barriers—they are guardrails for excellence.

Recognize Early Burnout Signals

Burnout rarely arrives suddenly—it whispers before it screams. Leaders who ignore the whispers pay the highest price. Watch for these early signals:

- **Cynicism replaces curiosity.** You stop asking questions and start assuming the worst.
- **Tasks expand because you avoid decisions.** Procrastination masquerades as productivity.
- **Sleep and joy shrink.** If your evenings bring only exhaustion, not renewal, your schedule is unsustainable.

Luxury leaders respond early. They adjust their rhythms, renegotiate commitments, and restore balance before the cost becomes irreversible.

Practical Example: The Executive Who Redefined Balance

A senior executive I worked with prided herself on being available 24/7. Her team admired her work ethic but quietly resented her lack of boundaries—because they mirrored it and burned out too. When her health declined, she finally embraced boundaries.

She implemented strict no-meeting zones, delegated decision rights more clearly, and treated recovery as part of her leadership strategy. Within 90 days, not only had her health improved, but her team had also become more autonomous, creative, and energized. By protecting her balance, she multiplied her team's performance.

Her lesson: *availability is not leadership; sustainability is.*

Power Prompts

- Which two boundaries, if enforced for 30 days, would change everything?
- What am I doing out of guilt that no longer serves the mission?
- If I modeled my current balance, would I want my team to copy it?

Final Word on Boundaries, Balance, and Burnout

Burnout prevention is not about slowing down—it is about lasting longer. Boundaries are not selfish—they are leadership. Balance is not indulgence—it is strategy.

When leaders cannot protect themselves, they unintentionally model unsustainable behaviors that ripple through the culture. When leaders honor boundaries, balance, and restoration, they model the excellence that compounds.

The goal is not just to build success—it is to sustain it. Leadership is not a sprint. It is a legacy.

CHAPTER 7

Decision-Making Under Pressure

The actual test of leadership is not how you perform when the path is clear—it is how you decide when the stakes are high, time is short, and information is incomplete. Prominent leaders do not always make perfect choices. Instead, they make **transparent choices**, act decisively, and correct quickly when reality shifts.

Indecision is often more damaging than a wrong decision. A team can adapt to a misstep, but it cannot adapt to paralysis. Luxury leaders understand that the weight of leadership is not about always being right—it is about being accountable, principled, and fast enough to keep momentum alive.

The 3-Lens Decision

Every major decision should be filtered through three lenses:

1. Principles — Alignment with Mission and Values

A decision that contradicts your organization's values may solve today's problem, but erode tomorrow's trust. Principles are the compass that prevents short-term wins from becoming long-term losses.

Mentor's Insight: Before saying yes, ask, "Will this still look honorable when retold five years from now?"

2. Proof — Data, Evidence, and Unknowns

Confidence without data is arrogance. But leaders must also accept that no decision comes with perfect information. The art lies in balancing available proof with the courage to act despite uncertainty.

Practice: Identify the 20% of data that drives 80% of clarity. Over-analysis is just a sophisticated form of procrastination.

1. People — Impact and Communication

Every decision touches someone. Who will be affected, and who must be informed? Ignoring this lens creates blind spots that later turn into resistance.

Luxury Leadership: Anticipate the ripple effect. Ask, *"Who will be disrupted by this choice, and how can I communicate with empathy while maintaining authority?"*

The R.A.P.I.D. Loop (Fast Cycle)

Under pressure, leaders need a system that keeps decisions both structured and fast. The **R.A.P.I.D. Loop** is a disciplined approach:

- **R — Reality:** Define the problem in one sentence. Ambiguity creates delay.
- **A — Alternatives:** Name at least three viable options. If there's only one option, you're not deciding—you're defaulting.
- **P — Payoffs:** Evaluate upsides, downsides, and second-order effects. What happens next quarter if we choose this? What unintended consequences might emerge?
- **I — Input:** Consult the two or three people closest to the facts, not the loudest voices in the room. Wisdom comes from proximity, not hierarchy.
- **D — Decide:** Time-box the decision. Set a review date. An action delayed is often an opportunity lost.

This loop forces momentum. It prevents endless debates and anchors decisions in principles, proof, and people.

Communicate Risk Like a Leader

The decision itself is only half the battle. The way you communicate it dictates if your team is confident or afraid. Vagueness creates rumors; clarity creates trust.

Luxury leaders explain decisions in a structured, transparent way:

- "We're choosing **Option B** for 60 days because_."
- "We will review on ____."
- "Success looks like __."
- "If X happens, we will pivot to C."

This method doesn't just share the decision—it shares the reasoning, the timeline, and the contingency plan. Organizations are secure not because all choices are flawless, but because every choice is open and responsible.

Practical Example: The Crisis Call

During a supply chain disruption, a retail CEO had to choose between delaying product launches and releasing with limited stock. Waiting for perfect certainty would have cost millions in lost sales.

With the R.A.P.I.D. Loop, the team rapidly assessed:

- **Reality:** Inventory levels were 40% below forecast.
- **Alternatives:** delay, partial launch, or substitute products.
- **Payoffs:** delay risked revenue; partial launch risked customer frustration; substitution risked brand perception.
- **Input:** Consulted logistics, finance, and marketing leads.
- **Decision:** Proceed with a partial launch for 60 days, while investing heavily in customer communication.

The CEO communicated risk clearly: "We're moving forward with a limited launch. Here's why. Here's how we'll support customers. Here's our pivot point if demand exceeds supply."

The decision wasn't flawless—but it was transparent, fast, and adaptive. Customers respected the honesty, employees trusted the leadership, and the company preserved momentum in a volatile season.

Power Prompts

- What decision am I stretching over weeks that could be made by Friday?
- What's the reversible version of this choice we can try now?
- If this decision is retold as a case study, will it highlight courage or hesitation?

Final Word on Decision-Making Under Pressure

Leadership is not about being fearless—it is about being responsible under fire. When pressure rises, the weak delay, the average guess, but the strong decide with principles, proof, and people in mind.

Legacy is not built on flawless choices—it is built on the courage to choose transparently, to act decisively, and to adapt when reality changes.

CHAPTER 8

Guiding Through Discord and Transition

C onflict avoided becomes conflict compounded. Change resisted becomes relevance lost. Both are unavoidable in leadership—and how you handle them determines whether your culture fractures or fortifies.

Luxury leaders do not fear conflict or resist change. Instead, they reframe both as catalysts for growth. Conflict, handled with precision, produces clarity and innovation. Change, led with discipline, ensures longevity and adaptability. Weak leaders react to conflict emotionally and approach change reluctantly. Powerful leaders turn both into opportunities to strengthen trust, align vision, and speed up progress.

Productive Conflict Rules

Conflict does not have to destroy relationships—it can refine them. But only if it's handled with structure and respect. Adopt these rules of productive conflict:

1. **Attack Problems, Not People**
   Keep focused on the issue, never the individual. Critique processes and behaviors, not character. This creates space for honesty without humiliation.

2. **Define Decision Rights Before Debate**
   Nothing fuels conflict like nuclear authority. Before the debate begins, clarify: *"Who ultimately owns this decision?"*

3. **Use Evidence, Not Volume**
   Raise your standards, not your voice. Decisions should rest on proof, not politics.

4. **End with Clarity**
   Every conflict must end with a decision, an owner, a deadline, and a follow-up. Otherwise, you are just rehearsing frustration.

The Change Ladder

Leaders often assume people resist change itself. People avoid change if they lack understanding, aren't ready, or cannot connect it to what they deem important. The

Change Ladder is a framework for guiding people through transition.

1. Explain Why Change Exists

Anchor the shift in market realities, mission needs, or margin goals. Vagueness breeds suspicion. Transparency builds trust.

2. Equip with Skills and Tools

Opposition decreases as people gain competence. Training, resources, and coaching turn anxiety into ability.

3. Enroll Early Adopters

Every culture has influencers. Enlist them early, model the new behavior, and let momentum spread.

4. Embed in Processes

Change is fragile until it's systematized. Bake it into SOPs, templates, and rituals so it survives beyond speeches.

5. Evaluate and Adjust

Measure impact, gather feedback, and refine continuously. Change is not a onetime event—it is an ongoing evolution.

Maintaining the Room during Difficult Seasons

If a struggle increases or alterations are challenging, the leader's presence is the steadying influence. Luxury leaders hold the room with composure and clarity:

- **Normalize Emotions, Anchor Behaviors.**
  Permit others to experience frustration or fear, while focusing on controlled deeds. Acknowledge emotion without letting it hijack progress.
- **Repeat the Vision, Shorten the Horizon.**
  When the time ahead is unsure, shorten the timeline. Say: *"This week, success means ___."* Certainty in the short term reduces panic in the long term.
- **Celebrate Progress Publicly, Coach Gaps Privately.**
  Public recognition fuels morale. Private correction protects dignity. Done consistently, this balancing preserves both culture and accountability.

Practical Example: Conflict that Created a Breakthrough

I once worked with a financial services firm where two senior leaders constantly clashed—one prioritizing client service, the other pushing aggressive growth. Meetings often ended in silence, with unresolved tension simmering beneath the surface.

We introduced the **Productive Conflict Rules.** Instead of debating personalities, they discussed strategies with data. Decision rights were clarified—marketing owned growth tactics, while client service owned delivery standards. Within weeks, what was once destructive conflict became productive tension, fueling innovation and improving both revenue and retention.

The lesson: conflict isn't the enemy. Mismanaged conflict is.

Practical Example: Change that Stuck

A mid-sized healthcare company needed to shift from paper to digital records. Staff resisted, fearing the new system would slow them down. Instead of forcing adoption, the CEO applied the Change Ladder.

- She explained *why* digitization was essential: compliance, patient safety, and faster care.
- She equipped the staff with one-on-one training and on-call support.
- Early adopters were recognized publicly as "efficiency supports."
- Processes were rewritten so that digital records weren't optional—they became the only system.
- Regular feedback sessions allowed staff to voice concerns and shape improvements.

The change was done in six months, and staff members showed more happiness because they were involved, backed, and esteemed.

Power Prompts

- What is the uncomfortable truth I need to say out loud?
- What behavior will we reward this quarter to make change stick?
- If conflict in my team escalates, will it reveal immaturity—or create innovation?

Final Word on Conflict and Change

Conflict and change are not detours from leadership—they are the terrain of leadership. To avoid them is to abandon your responsibility. Mastering them is to build resilience, trust, and adaptability into your culture.

Legacy leaders do not shy away from tension or transition. They embrace both as the very tools that forge strength, sharpen clarity, and create momentum that lasts.

CHAPTER 9

Building Teams That Thrive

Thriving teams are not accidents. They result from **intentional architecture**—designed, cultivated, and reinforced by leaders who understand that people don't just want a job; they want meaning, belonging, and growth.

Luxury leaders know this: a team that thrives will outperform a team that merely survives, not because they work harder, but because they work with clarity, alignment, and energy. Survival teams execute tasks. Thriving teams create momentum.

The Three Rs of Thriving Teams

1. Recruit for Alignment

Skills can be trained. Values cannot. Thriving teams begin with selecting people whose personal values align with the organization's culture. Selecting for talent can generate skill, although selecting for agreement creates dedication.

Mentor's Insight: When recruiting, ask questions that reveal not just what a candidate can do, but what they believe. A misaligned higher drain drains culture faster than a vacancy.

2. Role Clarity

Thriving teams don't guess what success looks like—they know. Clarity comes from role scorecards that outline outcomes, not just asks. Job descriptions describe chores. Scorecards define results.

Example: Instead of *"Manage customer service emails,"* define *"Reduce response time from 24 hours to 6 hours."* Outcomes empower people to innovate; chores box them into mediocrity.

3. Rituals that Create Momentum

Culture is shaped by what you repeat. Thriving teams have rituals that reinforce connection, alignment, and accountability, such as weekly 1:1s, project retrospectives, celebrating wins, or monthly strategy sessions. Rituals are the invisible rhythm that keeps the team pulsing with energy.

Scorecards, Not Job Descriptions

Traditional job descriptions often list endless responsibilities but rarely define impact. Thriving teams use **scorecards**:

- **Outcomes (3–5):** What measurable results must this role achieve?
- **Metrics:** How success will be tracked.

- **Resources:** What tools, budget, or support does the role require?
- **Rhythm:** How progress will be reviewed (weekly, biweekly, monthly).

When the outcome is clear, accountability becomes natural. Teams no longer debate effort—they measure results.

Grow Leaders, Not Dependents

Weak leaders hoard decisions, creating bottlenecks. Powerful leaders delegate outcomes, not tasks, so their people learn to think, not just to execute.

Luxury leaders coach with questions, not commands. Instead of giving answers, they ask:

- "What options do you see?"
- "What's your recommendation?"
- "What support do you need?"

This approach develops critical thinking, strengthens ownership, and produces future leaders instead of lifelong dependents.

Practical Example: From Dysfunction to Design

A mid-sized marketing agency struggled with constant turnover. Workers considered themselves overworked and underappreciated. When we analyzed the culture, we found no role clarity, inconsistent rituals, and leaders who micromanaged instead of coaching.

The agency rebuilt using the **Three Rs:**

- Recruited new hires with strong value alignment.
- Introduced scorecards so that every role had measurable outcomes.
- Instituted weekly "win sessions" to celebrate progress and monthly retros to refine the process.

Within a year, turnover dropped by 40%, revenue increased by 25%, and the culture shifted from burnout to breakthrough.

Practical Example: The Power of Delegation

A senior executive I mentored confessed that every decision, big or small, landed on her desk. Her team was paralyzed, waiting for her approval. Together, we implemented **outcome delegation**—assigning not just tasks, but ownership of results.

One manager was told: *"Your outcome is to increase client retention by 15%. I don't care how you do it—as long as it aligns with our values."* With autonomy, the manager developed new loyalty programs, improved onboarding, and exceeded the goal within six months.

The executive learned an elite truth: when you grow leaders instead of dependents, your influence multiplies.

Power Prompts

- If this role disappeared tomorrow, what value would the business immediately miss?
- Who on my team is ready for a stretch assignment, and what would it be?
- Do my people come to me with problems—or with solutions?

Final Word on Teams that Thrive

A thriving team is not built by chance—it is built by design. Recruitment aligned with values, clarity anchored in outcomes, and rituals that reinforce culture create momentum that sustains itself.

Legacy leaders know the goal is not just to build performers—it is to create leaders. Thriving teams outlast the founder, multiply the mission, and carry the culture forward long after the original leader has stepped away.

Teams don't thrive because of perks or paychecks. They thrive because of clarity, growth, and a leader who believes in them enough to demand excellence while providing the support to achieve it.

CHAPTER 10

Legacy Leadership: What Outlives You

S uccess is measured in achievements. Legacy is measured in what endures beyond you. Titles, accolades, and revenue may look impressive in the moment, but they fade quickly. True leaders think generationally. They ask not only, *"What did I build?"* but *"What did I leave behind that others can build upon?"*

Luxury leadership is not about personal visibility—it is about lasting impact. The highest mark of leadership is when your influence continues long after your presence.

From Operator to Orchestrator

Many leaders never graduate beyond operator mode—constantly deciding, solving problems, and ensuring things get done. But if the organization depends entirely on your presence, you have not built a legacy—you have built a liability.

To move from operator to orchestrator, commit to three practices:

1. **Build Playbooks That Work Without You**

   A true leader designs systems, not bottlenecks—document not only the *what* but also the *how* and the *why*. A playbook transforms expertise into repeatable excellence.

2. **Document Decisions, Not Just Tasks**

   Most organizations record processes but rarely capture decision logic. Document *why* choices were made, not just *what* was done. This allows future leaders to understand principles, not just procedures.

3. **Identify and Mentor Successors Now**

   A leader who cannot mentor successors is a leader planning for collapse. Identify potential leaders early, stretch them with responsibility, and mentor them through mistakes. Legacy is not built when you leave—it is built in the leaders you raise before you leave.

The Legacy Flywheel

Sustainable leadership operates like a flywheel—a cycle that strengthens with every rotation:

Principles → Playbooks → People → Progress → Refined Principles.

You begin with values, convert them into documented systems, empower people to execute them, measure progress, and then refine your principles with what you've learned. Each turn of the flywheel makes the organization stronger, more consistent, and less dependent on a single leader.

This is how legacies are engineered—not in grand gestures, but in disciplined cycles that build resilience.

Make It Bigger Than You

Legacy is never about ego—it is about expansion. If everything begins and ends with you, the mission is too small. Luxury leaders intentionally make their vision bigger than themselves:

1. **Invest in Leaders Who differ from You**

   Diversity is not cosmetic—it is catalytic. Seek leaders who don't look like you, think like you, or agree with you. They stretch the culture, expand the perspective, and ensure the organization strengthens beyond one person's worldview.

2. **Tie Profit to Purpose in Tangible Ways**

   Purpose without action is marketing. Tie your resources to initiatives that outlive you: scholarships, leadership pipelines, or community partnerships. When profit fuels purpose, legacy becomes visible.

Practical Example: The Founder Who Let Go

A successful entrepreneur I coached struggled with succession. His team relied on him for every critical decision, and he feared letting go would reduce quality. But when he finally began documenting playbooks, empowering his managers, and mentoring a successor, something remarkable happened—his company not only survived without him for 90 days, it thrived.

Clients saw improved response times, employees were more trusted, and profits grew. The entrepreneur realized: *"My true legacy isn't what I control—it's what I release."*

Power Prompts

- If I vanished for 90 days, what would break? That's my next system.
- What is the narrative my team will give about my influence on their emotions, development, and victory?
- Am I building something that ends with me—or something that expands beyond me?

Final Word on Legacy Leadership

Success is what you can claim. Legacy is what others can continue. To lead for legacy is to build systems that endure, empower leaders who multiply, and invest in missions that matter of profit.

Luxury leaders do not simply chase success—they design permanence. They understand that the most accurate measure of leadership is not applause in the present, but impact in the future.

Your leadership will either vanish with you or it will outlive you. The choice is yours.

Conclusion

Built for Legacy

L eadership is not a moment. It is not a title. It is not the applause of today. Leadership is a **daily choice**—to live aligned with your values, to decide clearly even under pressure, to speak truthfully even when uncomfortable, and to serve generously even when it costs you.

When you lead yourself first—your time, your emotions, your habits, and your standards—you become the person others instinctively trust to lead anything else. Trust is not granted with position—it is earned through consistency. Titles don't create leaders. Habits do.

The leaders who build legacies understand this:

- They go first. Not when it's convenient, but when it's costly.
- They tell the truth sooner. Because delay erodes trust faster than mistakes ever could.
- They decide faster. Because momentum compounds when hesitation is removed.
- They build others higher. Because legacy is not about personal success—it is about creating success in others.

Your journey of leadership begins with self-mastery, but it cannot end there. It must expand outward—to your team, your organization, your industry, and your community. The ripple effect of your habits, your courage, and your clarity will shape cultures, transform lives, and outlive your name.

The choice before you is simple yet profound: Will you chase temporary success, or will you design a legacy that endures?

Lead yourself with discipline. Lead others with vision. Lead your world with impact.

Lead yourself first—then lead everything else.

Thank you for reading. We've included a free downloadable workbook to help you apply these principles. **Scan for FREE WORKBOOK printable tracker & digital copy**

Next Steps

From Knowledge to Action

This book's end wasn't the goal—it was the beginning. You now hold frameworks, principles, and strategies that can transform the way you lead. But transformation only happens when insight becomes implementation.

Here's how to take the following steps:

1. **Choose One Daily Habit**

   Leadership compounds in small, repeated actions. Select one habit from this book—whether it's the morning clarity check, the C.A.L.M. method, or the 4C communication model—and commit to practicing it consistently for 30 days. Mastery begins with one step.

2. **Run a 90-Day Sprint**

   Don't change everything at once. Pick one area—vision, culture, or decision-making—and apply a 90-day sprint. Measure progress, adjust as needed, and lock in the wins before moving on.

3. **Mentor Someone Immediately**

Legacy begins the moment you invest in others. Share one framework from this book with someone you lead. Walk them through it, and let them practice it. Teaching multiplies impact.

4. Design Your Legacy Blueprint

Write what you want outlived—what systems, what people, what principles. Then ask yourself, *"What am I building today that ensures this exists tomorrow?"*

5. Stay in Motion

The greatest threat to leadership is not failure—it is stagnation. Keep moving, keep deciding, keep refining. Leadership is not about perfection; it's about momentum.

Your Legacy Starts Now

The leaders who build legacies are not the ones who wait for permission. They are the ones who take what they know, act on it, and adjust along the way.

You don't need more time. You don't need more titles. You need courage to start—right here, right now.

Go first. Decide today. Build what will outlive you.

Booked & Branded Publishing

About the Author

Stephanie Williams, MBA — Strategic Business Consultant, author, and builder of beauty, brains, and business.

Stephanie Williams is a powerhouse in strategy, leadership, and transformation. With a perfect GPA from the prestigious Jack Welch Management Institute, where she earned her MBA with a concentration in entrepreneurship, Stephanie has built her career helping individuals and organizations turn vision into results.

From her success in corporate sales at Verizon to founding Booked & Branded Publishing, a luxury ghostwriting and publishing firm, Stephanie has consistently proven her ability to lead, execute, and scale. Her work spans industries — from real estate and trucking to skincare and leadership — reflecting both her business acumen and her passion for empowering others to reach their next level.

In Glow Up Leadership: Lead Yourself First, Then Lead Everything Else, Stephanie combines her real-world experience with a relatable, motivational voice that makes leadership accessible without watering it down. She believes authentic leadership starts with self-mastery — building confidence, clarity, and consistency — and then flows into every team, project, or business you touch.

Through her books, coaching, and publishing company, Stephanie's mission is simple: to help leaders glow from the inside out, leading lives and organizations that are not only successful, but sustainable, authentic, and impactful.

Stephanie lives by the mantra: "Where hustle meets strategy." This philosophy fuels both her personal journey and her mission to empower others to build legacies with purpose, clarity, and impact.

Thank you for your purchase. I'd appreciate it if you could write a short Amazon review, assuming this book has been helpful. Your words help others find this message and remind them they are not alone.

Scan QR Code to leave a review on Amazon.

Work With Me

You've just invested in your leadership by finishing this book. Now imagine taking what you know and translating it into assets that multiply your impact—books, frameworks, and systems that outlive you. That's where I come in.

If you're ready to:

- **Turn your expertise into a premium book** that cements your authority and expands your influence.
- **Build a leadership program or intellectual property suite** that trains others in your frameworks.

Systematize your business for scale so it runs with excellence even when you step away — I'd love to help you make it happen.

At **Booked and Branded Publishing**, we specialize in transforming leaders into legacies through:

- **High-Velocity Ghostwriting.**
  Books crafted with executive-level clarity, written quickly without sacrificing luxury or authority.
- **Luxury-Level Workbooks & IP Frameworks.**
  Tools your team and clients can use to implement your methods of precision.
- **Brand and Go-to-Market Systems.**
  Strategies that turn your thought leadership into revenue, recognition, and reach.

This isn't about creating content—it's about creating an asset that positions you as the voice in your space.

Explore packages and book a private consultation today.

www.bookedandbrandedpublishing.com

Tagline: *Where hustle meets strategy.*

Appendix — Leader Tools & Templates

A. 30/60/90 Plan (Template)

- 30 Days: Orient, baseline, quick wins (list 3)
- 60 Days: Build—ship improved process (list 2).
- 90 Days: Scale—document playbook, train owner(s).

B. Weekly Leadership Review (15 Minutes)

- Wins: What moved the mission?
- Risks: What needs a decision?
- People: Who needs coaching or recognition?
- Process: What will I simplify this week?

C. Difficult Conversation Script

1. Open with standard care.
2. Describe behavior and impact (facts).
3. Ask for their view.
4. Agree on next step, deadline, and support.
5. Document and follow up.

www.ingramcontent.com/pod-product-compliance
Lightning Source LLC
Chambersburg PA
CBHW021718210326
41599CB00013B/1689